CAREERS INSIDE THE WORLD OF
Sales

D1411582

Salespeople are the connection between a business and the consumer.

CAREERS & OPPORTUNITIES

CAREERS INSIDE THE WORLD OF

Sales

by Carlienne Frisch

THE ROSEN PUBLISHING GROUP, INC.
NEW YORK

Published in 1995, 1998 by The Rosen Publishing Group, Inc.
29 East 21st Street, New York, NY 10010

Revised 1998

Library of Congress Cataloging-in-Publication Data

Frisch, Carlienne, 1944–
    Careers inside the world of sales / by Carlienne Frisch.
        p.   cm — (The library of social activism)
    Includes bibliographical references and index.
    ISBN 0-8239-2738-5
    1. Selling—Vocational guidance—Juvenile literature. [1. Selling—
Vocational guidance. 2. Vocational guidance. 3. Occupations.] I. Title.
II.Series.
HF5438.25.F77   1995
658.85'023'73—dc20   95-22143
                                                        CIP
                                                        AC

Manufactured in the United States of America

Contents

Sales positions are found in many different arenas. One of the most vital
areas of sales is the fashion industry.

CHAPTER 1

CAREERS IN SALES

Have you ever thought about working in retail sales? Maybe the idea of working in a clothing or music store sounds as if it might be fun and a good way to earn some extra money.

Or perhaps you already have some sales experience and are considering making sales your career. But what kind of opportunities, responsibilities, and money can you expect from a careers in sales?

You may be curious about the types of sales careers that are available. Although you may be familiar with some positions, such as salesperson and cashier, there are also many behind-the-scenes jobs, like buyer and sales manager. There are also specialized fields, such as insurance or real estate sales. Or are you interested in a sales-related career such as advertising agent or marketing executive?

In this book, we will explore these and other jobs inside the world of sales.

What Is a Sales Career?

Sales is the link between the world of business and the consumer. Businesses do one of two things. They either make products, such as computers or clothing, or they provide services like haircuts or tennis lessons and offer them for sale. Consumers then buy and use these products and services. Salespeople help to make this exchange between businesses and consumers happen.

There are many types of sales careers depending on what products are sold and how the consumers are reached. These careers include retail sales, marketing, advertising, specialty sales, and direct sales.

• Retail salespeople work in stores and shops. Anytime you buy something from a store you are participating in retail. These salespeople sell food, clothing, furniture, and just about anything else you might buy for yourself or your home.

• People involved in marketing work for wholesalers. Marketers help wholesalers sell their products to stores rather than individual people. Other marketers may promote the use of a sports arena or distribute product samples in a store. Telemarketers sell products or services over the phone.

• Advertising salespeople sell advertising space for businesses in newspapers and magazines or

The most successful salespeople are sincere and friendly but persistent.

on commercial television and radio. There are also those who work in advertising agencies creating ads for businesses.

• Specialty salespeople include real estate agents, investment advisers, and insurance agents. Someone involved in specialty sales might represent a company that produces advanced or hi-tech machinery. This person might make presentations to explain the company's product and the services that go along with it.

• Direct sales involve a salesperson going door to door to demonstrate a product in customers' homes. A direct salesperson may demonstrate and sell Tupperware at a "party" hosted by a customer.

A direct salesperson may also go door to door selling encyclopedias.

What Does It Take to Be a Sales Professional?

Successful salespeople have certain characteristics. They enjoy being at the center of activity. They know everything about the products and services they sell. Good salespeople can persuade customers to buy by providing appealing facts about their products or services. They are also able to compare their products to similar products and convince the consumer that their products are the best.

The most successful salespeople are sincere, friendly, and helpful. They must be persistent and determined, but must also persuade customers to buy without being "pushy."

Enthusiasm is important in catching a customer's interest in a product. Successful salespeople are eager to tell customers about new products or services that might interest them.

Salespeople must also be "self-starters." They need to work hard without having anyone tell them to do so. Many people in sales jobs must be willing to work long hours including evenings and weekends.

Salespeople should also believe in the product or service being sold. Many people are able to recognize when salespeople are phony or "feeding them a line." Few will do business with salespeople who don't seem honest.

Successful salespeople need to have good speech and language skills. They must be able to communicate clearly with customers. Someone who is shy or does not like meeting people will probably not want a career in sales.

Many of today's salespeople find it necessary to have an education beyond that of a high school graduate. Vocational schools, business colleges, community colleges, and universities have many programs to study and learn about marketing, advertising, real estate, and business.

How Do Sales Professions Differ?

Sales careers have many things in common. But because there are so many kinds of sales jobs, they also have many differences. The kind of job you may get depends on your interests, your abilities, and the opportunities in the area where you live.

Retail sales workers usually live near the store where they work. Marketing specialists often work in cities or large towns. They sometimes travel to sell in other cities or states. Telemarketers may work entirely from home: All they need is telephone equipment. Advertising representatives live and work wherever advertising is sold—

Some companies require their salespeople to travel. Several computer companies, including IBM and Apple Computers, were represented at a semiannual computer show in Chicago. Salespeople were present to show potential customers their new products.

in major cities and in towns with only a few hundred people. A specialty salesperson may work for a real estate agency in a small town. Another may travel through many states selling insurance programs to large corporations. People in direct sales usually work in their own community.

Salespeople have varied hours of work. A part-time retail clerk may work fifteen hours a week. A marketing specialist may spend many hours each week just driving from one appointment to another.

The pay range for salespeople is wide. Retail salesworkers usually earn an hourly wage. They often begin at the minimum wage and get small raises over time.

Some salespeople work on commission, which means that they get a percentage of each sale. Mary Horton sells cosmetics on a 40 percent commission. For every $100 of cosmetics Mary sells, she receives $40. When she sells $500 of cosmetics in one week, her commission is $200. But if she sells only $200 in a week, her income is only $80. Some companies believe that selling on commission gives workers an incentive, a reason to work harder. But many salespeople dislike the pressure of working only on commission. They want the security of a regular salary.

Some salespeople receive a small base salary along with commissions. This gives them some security along with incentive to try for a bigger commission. The most successful salespeople often receive a bonus, an amount of money for making exceptionally large sales or being the top producer in a company or department during a certain time period.

Full-time salespeople usually receive fringe benefits such as paid vacations and medical insurance. Some employers also offer paid sick leave and life insurance. Retail workers usually receive a discount on purchases. Self-employed salesworkers do not receive fringe benefits, and they must pay self-employment tax (like Social Security tax) to the government.

The Responsibilities of Sales

Selling is a form of communication. The salesperson must explain the products or services and how they can be used. The salesperson also must learn or guess what the customer wants, how the customer plans to use the product or service, and how much money the customer is willing to spend.

A successful salesperson has learned to ask the customer questions and to listen carefully to the answers. Customers cannot be forced to buy a product or service they do not want. A salesperson must use information about the product or service along with persuasion based on the customer's answers.

What You Can Do Now

You can find out whether you enjoy sales while still in school by getting part-time or summer work in a store. In most states, you must be sixteen years old to get a job.

You also can gain sales experience at your school's newspaper, yearbook, or booster club. If your school has a DECA (Distributive Education Clubs of America) chapter, join it. Teachers advise DECA members in making and selling products. Students develop sales skills and learn about financing, pricing, sales planning, competition, promotion, and marketing.

You can gain experience in sales by getting a part-time or summer job in a local store.

Questions to Ask Yourself

There are many different opportunities in the world of sales. You have to decide which career is right for you. 1) Which of the sales opportunities described in this chapter do you find interesting? 2) What personality characteristics does a salesperson need? Do you have those characteristics? 3) Salespeople are paid in several ways. Do you want a steady income with some opportunity for a raise or for advancement? Or would you rather have a small salary and earn the rest of your income in commissions and bonuses? Why?

CHAPTER 2

RETAIL SALES

Consumers buy most products through retail sales. A retail salesperson learns about customers' tastes, attitudes, and desires. Good retail salespeople usually are quickly promoted into marketing, management, or other retail jobs.

Retailing is a large and varied field. About 25 million people sell about $2.3 trillion in retail goods each year in the United States. Average sales per salesperson are more than $92,000 annually, but individual sales vary greatly.

A post-high school education is often helpful, but not always necessary. Most medium-sized and large retailers offer long-term training programs for beginners. Supervisors and managers provide on-the-job training that may include some classes.

Retail salespeople work in department stores, discount stores, specialty stores, and small shops and boutiques. Service to the customer is what all retail salespeople must provide.

A stylish appearance, an interest in fashion, and an outgoing personality all help a retail salesperson to be successful.

Retail Clothing Sales

Kerri Cox is a retail sales associate. She works in the high-fashion section of Herberger's, a department store. Kerri applied for a clothing sales job while in high school. Her attractive appearance, interest in fashion, outgoing personality, and ability to deal with a variety of people helped her get the job. Even after graduation, Kerri worked many evenings and weekends before she got a better schedule.

"I enjoy helping people choose just the right outfit and accessories," Kerri says. "I answer questions about the clothing's care and construc-   17 tion. I have to know which styles and sizes are available in various price ranges, and how one article of clothing compares with another. I like doing this. What I don't like is complaints from customers. Some people think prices are too high, especially if they bought an outfit that went on sale a week later."

Retail sales people earn $10,000 to $24,000 a year, depending on experience, commission, price range of the merchandise, and number of hours worked. Kerri's favorite fringe benefit is the 25 percent discount she gets on any merchandise in the store—clothing, cosmetics, housewares.

The turnover is high in retail sales, so there are many opportunities. You can get experience by working part time, especially during the Christmas season. If you are good at sales, you can advance quickly.

Clothing Buyer

Peggy Daley worked as a salesperson in a Midwestern retail chain while in college. She was quickly promoted to sportswear department manager, supervising salespeople and advising the teen fashion board. Peggy's university education in marketing, management, and economics, combined with her great fashion sense, helped her become a buyer two years later. Some buyers train on the job.

"Clothing buyers must know fashion trends and their store's customers' preferences," Peggy says. "I make eight or nine buying trips to New York each year. There I go to fashion shows and scout the fashion houses. I bring back the looks I think will catch on in the Midwest. Then I help our sales-people price and promote the clothes. If I buy too many items that sell poorly, I could get fired."

Buyers must adjust to many people and situations. Peggy's style on a buying trip depends on what kind of person she is meeting. She can change from hyper to laid back, from dramatic to conservative, and from assertive to charming.

Buyers earn $20,000 to $45,000 a year, depending on their location, length of employment, and the store's sales volume.

Other Retail Fashion Careers

Most fashion retail careers require an outgoing personality, some fashion sense, and an ability to be flexible. To find out whether fashion retailing suits you, apply for a spot on a store's teen fashion advisory board, read fashion magazines, and work part time or summers in a clothing store.

If you are successful in retail sales, you may get a job training other people in sales. Retail sales experience and a good sense of fashion prepare you to be a fashion consultant or personal

Sales managers often have experience in marketing, advertising,
merchandise display, and personnel management.

shopper for busy customers. A person with this job chooses a collection of clothing and accessories each season for a customer to approve and buy.

Sales Management

Sales management requires a variety of experience. A sales manager in a store or in a single department is responsible for promoting merchandise and setting sales goals. The manager supervises sales associates and makes sure customers are satisfied with the merchandise and the salespeople. Sales managers also plan a budget and follow it to control expenses.

Many sales managers have a college degree. They have education and experience in accounting, merchandise display, marketing, advertising, and personnel management (hiring, firing, and managing employees). Some managers take a shorter program at a vocational school or community college and then learn on the job. Sales managers earn $24,000 to $45,000 annually.

Retail Store Ownership

Some store owners buy merchandise such as books, hobby supplies, or jewelry from wholesalers. The retail owner must sell the products at a price that pays for the merchandise and the costs of operating the store. These include rent, electricity, heat, insurance, wages of any employees, and a salary for the owner. The pressure of these financial responsibilities can be stressful.

A consignment shop is another kind of retail store. In some communities, you can get a permit to operate a consignment shop from your home or garage. People bring you items they want to sell. You sell the items and keep part of the money from each sale. There is no start-up cost for inventory.

Before opening a consignment shop, you must advertise for consignees, the people who bring merchandise to sell. You should sign a contract with each consignee, listing the consignment, how long you will keep it, what you will do with unsold merchandise, and what percentage of the sales price you will retain. Consignment shops often keep half of the sales price.

Your chance of success in a consignment shop depends on your knowledge of customers' tastes and of the merchandise. Depending on your interests, you might want to sell locally made craft items, used books, or used sports equipment. A clothing consignment shop may carry recent styles of clothing in good condition, jewelry, and vintage (old) clothing appropriate for costumes.

People who operate a retail store must be tactful and pleasant. They promote the store by word of mouth and with advertisements. They are confident enough to make important decisions and to direct the work of any employees they hire. They need energy for waiting on customers and moving merchandise around the store. Math skills are important for keeping records of merchandise, prices, and sales.

A self-employed retailer cannot count on a certain level of income. But the retailer has the freedom and responsibility of making business decisions. Shop owners can make $10,000 to $40,000 or more yearly, depending on the size of the community. They must provide their own medical insurance and pay self-employment tax and income tax from their profits.

If you hope to own a consignment or other retail store, you should work in one first. Take classes in accounting and merchandising. Ask a librarian to help you find trade magazines that interest you. Examples include *Bicycle Business Journal*, *Book Dealers World*, *Fashion Accessories*, and *Model Railroader*.

Sales Clerk/Cashier

Not all sales work involves risk or stress. Joan Miller is a sales clerk, or cashier, who waits on customers at a Lucky Food Store. Joan spends six hours on her feet behind a checkout counter. As customers unload their groceries, Joan moves each item across the electronic scanner that enters its price in the cash register's computer. The computer shows the total amount of the

Cashiers often have low-stress sales jobs.

sale. When the customer pays Joan, she punches the computer keys for that amount. The computer then shows the amount of change due. Joan gives the customer the change and bags the groceries.

Cashiers usually need only a high school education, but they must be able to do the same work for several hours without getting bored. They also need good hand coordination and the math skills to make change without a computer. Customers expect cashiers to be friendly, helpful, and efficient.

Most cashiers begin work at minimum wage. **24** With regular raises over time, they may double their wage rate. Cashiers are needed in grocery stores, convenience stores, gasoline stations, discount stores, and in many small retail businesses.

Questions to Ask Yourself

If you have decided on a career in sales, you need to decide which of the many possible careers is best for you. 1) In which sales careers are math skills important? Can you think of sales jobs where math is not needed? 2) Which sales jobs involve evening and weekend work? How would you feel about these jobs if you had a family? If you were single? 3) Which sales jobs seem to have the most security? Which seem to be the most stressful? Which of these jobs appeals to you and why?

CHAPTER 3

MARKETING

Marketing specialists have many career choices. A telemarketer sells products and services over the phone. Telemarketers may work from home or at a "phone bank" surrounded by many other people doing the same work.

A product marketer sells to wholesalers, buyers, retailers, or directly to consumers. Some product marketers take a booth at trade fairs; others have a booth in the local supermarket.

Mail order marketers may work out of their home, a warehouse, or an office. Some marketing jobs combine sales with public relations.

Telemarketing

"Hello, Mrs. Jones, I'm Mary Brown. How are you today?" In this telephone conversation, Mary gives her planned sales pitch, telling Mrs. Jones about a new travel plan that will save the Jones family hundreds of dollars on each trip they charge on their credit card.

Mary is telemarketing. *Business Week* magazine estimates that by the year 2000, there will be more than eight million jobs in telemarketing.

Sometimes when Mrs. Jones receives a telemarketing call, she hangs up. Sometimes she listens and says, "No, thank you." But sometimes she agrees to buy what the telemarketer is selling. Mrs. Jones's response depends largely on the telemarketer's ability to be persuasive and provide information. But it is also affected by Mrs. Jones's mood that day and her interest in the product or service.

Appearance can be a plus in many sales jobs, but it doesn't matter in telemarketing. You should have a pleasant, friendly voice and speak clearly.

Successful telemarketers must be able to sit in one place for a long period of time. They keep their work organized. They set sales goals and manage their time carefully. They use the telephone as a professional tool.

Telemarketers must build rapport and trust with the person on the other end of the phone. They must ask the right questions and listen carefully to the answers. They must be able to handle objections without arguing. They also must be able to answer many questions about the product or service they are selling. Many companies provide training when they hire new telemarketers.

Many people hang up on a telemarketer. A telemarketer must not take that personally. A

Telemarketers must build rapport and trust with the person on the other end of the phone.

good self-image and strong ego are important. If you are confident, enjoy talking on the phone, and have a talent for sales, a career in telemarketing could be for you.

The pay for telemarketers varies greatly. Many telemarketers are paid an hourly wage and earn about $10,000 a year. Some telemarketers who sell to businesses rather than private consumers can earn $70,000 a year in salary and commissions.

Product Marketing

Steve Stein markets cheese and other dairy products to supermarkets and grocery stores for Dairyland Foods. Steve is friendly, businesslike, and well groomed. Each workday he visits several of his customers. He drives nearly 3,000 miles a month in his company car.

"Product marketing is very competitive," Steve says. "I follow a schedule to meet with each supermarket's buyer. This is the person who buys the merchandise the store carries. Dairyland's products compete for shelf space with our competitors' products."

At each store, Steve tells the buyer about the Dairyland products that will be available in the coming months and how Dairyland will advertise the products. Sometimes he arranges for a demonstrator to promote the products in the store with samples and coupons.

"I also show the buyer new products, such as

low-fat Swiss cheese and a yogurt-cereal snack," Steve says. "I suggest ways to display the products to catch the customer's eye."

In the evening, Steve does paperwork at home. He uses his personal computer to send the orders to the computer at Dairyland's main office. Although Steve can arrange his own schedule, he must visit each of his customers during each product promotion. Some buyers expect to see him on a certain day of the week. During special promotions, work takes up almost all of Steve's time.

Steve's college degree in speech and psychology helps him "read" a customer's personality, listen carefully, and speak well. Product marketers usually have some education after high school. They may take a two-year marketing program at a vocational-technical school or community college. Many product marketers have a bachelor's degree, usually in sales and marketing.

Opportunities for product marketers are expected to grow. Earnings range from $20,000 to $30,000 a year, depending on experience, type of market, and location. Some product marketers work on commissions, with no salary; many receive bonuses. With additional business education, a product marketer can advance into a management job.

If product marketing interests you, talk with the food sales representatives who visit supermarkets in your area. Get a part-time or summer job in a grocery store and see how the store handles product displays and promotions. You should study English, business, math, and communications. Psychology and computer courses also are helpful. You can learn about competition in debates, math competitions, or competitive sports. Ask a librarian to get you copies of magazines such as *Candy Wholesaler* and *The Food Channel.*

Product Demonstration

Karen Palmer prepares and hands out food samples in supermarkets three days a week. Karen is a product demonstrator. She promotes new products or products that are on sale.

A product demonstrator needs a pleasant personality, an attractive appearance, and the ability to stand in one place for many hours. Most supermarkets schedule product promotions on weekends, when the store is busiest. Demonstrators usually work 15 to 25 hours from Friday through Sunday.

"I must know how to prepare each food I promote," Karen explains. "If I'm preparing pizza or fish, I use a toaster oven or electric skillet. I could use the store's cooking equipment, but I prefer to bring my own from home. I enjoy meeting people and answering their questions about the food's nutritional value and preparation."

A product demonstrator may be hired and trained by a supermarket manager. Some work for a "demo service" that provides training.

The need for product demonstrators is

A product demonstrator needs a pleasant personality, a neat appearance, and the ability to gain the attention of potential customers.

expected to grow. Demonstrators earn between minimum wage and $10 an hour, depending on location and employer. Courses in home economics, speech, and sales are helpful.

If you are interested in product demonstration, talk to demonstrators in local supermarkets. You might ask a store manager to let you work as a demonstrator during the summer.

Demonstration Management

If you enjoy teaching people, making arrangements over the phone, and keeping good records, you might start your own demo service. That's what Margaret Brent did after she had worked as a demonstrator. She had experience and the ability to get along with many kinds of people. Courses in home economics, accounting, and speech helped her succeed.

"I started my business at home, using a telephone and typewriter," Margaret says. "I sent letters to all the supermarket managers who knew me, offering to provide trained demonstrators for a fee. Then I recruited a few neighbors and trained them. Soon I had requests from so many supermarkets that I had to advertise for people to train as demonstrators."

A few years later, Margaret's demo service had 100 part-time demonstrators under contract. Margaret and her partner schedule each week's demos and assign the demonstrators. They collect a fee from each supermarket. The demonstrators are paid directly by the supermarket or by the food company whose product is promoted. The demo service made a profit of $36,000 last year. Margaret and her partner each took a salary of $12,000.

Public Relations/Marketing

Your team just made a home run or a touchdown. You jump to your feet and scream with joy, along with thousands of other people in the stadium. Later, you wonder what it's like behind the scenes, after the screaming fans go home.

Are you interested in sports? Do you work well

with people? Can you keep details organized? If you answered yes, you might enjoy working as a stadium marketing and public relations director, like Mike Brown. You must also understand statistics, communicate clearly, and be persuasive. You should work well alone or as part of a team.

Mike has many responsibilities with the Winona Hawks. He provides statistical and game reports to radio, television, newspaper, and magazine reporters. He arranges interviews for the team's players. Mike also sells advertising to local businesses for the team's radio and TV game broadcasts, stadium billboards, printed game programs, and yearbook.

When the team is away from home, Mike works with other people to schedule events in the stadium such as a rock concert or a religious crusade. He also arranges contracts for souvenirs, food and beverages, stadium maintenance, and cleanup.

A job like Mike's pays $10,000 to $25,000 or more a year, depending on the team's league level and the advertising success.

To prepare for a career like Mike's, study communications, English, statistics, marketing, public relations, advertising, psychology, and business. Experience in high school sports is a plus. Talk with workers in the office of a college or professional sports team. Try to get a part-time or summer job in the office or as a member of a

A stadium marketing and public relations director often works to book other types of entertainment to keep the stands filled.

stadium work crew. Try reporting on your sports team for your school newspaper. Sell advertising for the yearbook. If sports don't interest you but public relations does, consider promoting a theater, a university student center, or a business.

Questions to Ask Yourself

There are many possible careers in marketing. You have to decide if any of these careers suit you. 1) Can you take an abrupt no without feeling hurt? 2) Could you take charge of an entire line of products? 3) Would you be willing to invest time and money in college to qualify for a job?

CHAPTER 4

ADVERTISING SALES

There are many kinds of jobs in advertising sales. Some people sell time for commercials on radio or television. Others sell advertising space in newspapers, magazines, or newsletters. Some people work for advertising agencies.

People who sell advertising are called sales executives or account executives. The "executive" title usually means that they manage the advertising for their customers. In advertising jobs, customers are called accounts or clients.

Advertising Agencies

Ramon Banos is an account executive at an advertising agency. He is responsible for several accounts.

Ramon depends on the agency's market researchers to tell him what kind of customers are interested in a client's products. With this information, Ramon designs an advertising campaign, or plan, to sell the client's products.

The campaign may include advertising in several media, such as television, radio, magazines, newspapers, or newsletters. Sometimes Ramon recommends direct-mail advertising—sending advertisements to the homes or businesses of potential customers.

Ramon then must "sell" the advertising campaign to the client. If the client agrees to pay for the campaign, Ramon works with other people in the agency to produce the advertisements and to place them in the media.

The demand for advertising account executives continues to grow as business competition increases. An advertising account executive earns $20,000 to $50,000 or more a year, depending on location and the size of the agency.

If you are interested in a job like Ramon's, you should take courses in marketing, business, advertising, and communications. You need a high level of creativity. You can gain experience by creating and selling advertising for your school newspaper or yearbook. Cut out advertisements you like, including those that arrive in the mail, and keep a file. Ask a librarian for magazines such as *Advertising Age* and *Marketing Media and Decisions*.

Television and Radio Account Sales

Television and radio stations would go out of business without account executives like Gina

Woods. Gina sells commercial air time on WLS radio in Chicago. The money from advertising pays for the station's employees—disc jockeys, news announcers, and account executives.

"I call on my accounts frequently with new ideas for ads," Gina says. "Sometimes I help them create jingles to sell their products or services. I help clients choose the best air times for their advertising and arrange the times at WLS. I also prepare the contracts my clients sign. I keep written records of all my accounts."

Gina spends much of her day in her car, driving from one account to another. When she has time, she makes cold calls, trying to interest new advertisers in WLS. She prepares proposals to convince prospective advertisers that WLS will get better results for them than other Chicago stations. Gina also creates promotions for grand openings, holidays, and slow business times.

"I have to be aggressive, confident, well organized, and creative," Gina explains. "To handle this fast-paced job, you must work well under pressure and have a high energy level. It's important not to take a client's rejection personally."

Advertising people consider radio and television sales the most glamorous jobs. There are many opportunities, but competition is tough at larger stations. Account executives earn $20,000 to $50,000 or more, depending on

Advertising salespeople sell air time on radio and television stations as well as ads in print media.

their experience, the station's size, and the area's business climate. Many account executives are paid commissions only.

To prepare for a job like Gina's, talk with a sales executive at a local radio station. Try to get a part-time job at a station to learn how it operates. Get sales experience at a store or by handling sales promotions such as homecoming buttons at school. Listen to radio ads and analyze them. Take courses in English, speech, business, and psychology. College education is helpful, especially courses in marketing, advertising, communications, and business. It is also important for advancement into management positions.

Print Advertising Sales

Although people pay for the newspapers and
magazines they read, it is advertising that pays
for most of the costs. Advertising representatives
(ad reps) sell space in newspapers, magazines, or
newsletters. They find new accounts by calling
people and businesses that advertise in other
publications. Some ad reps meet new clients
by attending business activities such as local
Chamber of Commerce events.

Megan O'Reilly is a newspaper ad rep in
New Jersey. She sells and creates advertising for a
few large accounts and several small businesses.
Each week, Megan reviews her clients' past and
current advertising. She asks clients what product
or service they want to promote. Megan writes
the ad copy (the words that will sell the product).
She designs the ad layout (the way the ad will
look) and takes it to the newspaper's production
department to be printed. She shows a printed
sample of the ad to her accounts to get their
approval.

Deadlines can create pressure and stress.
Megan is responsible if there is a problem with
an ad. Some ad reps also collect payment from
their accounts.

Newspaper ad reps earn $15,000 to $40,000 a
year in base salary and commissions. Newsletter
advertising incomes are similar. Magazine advertising incomes may be higher.

Taking business classes like accounting can help you prepare for a career in print sales.

If you have a way with words and a good eye for detail, you may do well in print advertising sales. You must be self-disciplined and willing to work long hours. You should be outgoing, ambitious, enthusiastic, and persuasive. You must work well with others, yet be able to work alone.

Previous sales experience is helpful. A college degree in marketing, advertising, communications, or a related field is strongly recommended, especially for advertising representatives who hope to advance to upper management.

To prepare for a job like Megan's, talk with an   **41**

advertising representative. Get a part-time job (or work as a volunteer) at a newspaper. Sell ads and design pages for your school newspaper, magazine, or yearbook. Take courses in English, photography, graphic arts, speech, communications, marketing, psychology, and business.

Questions to Ask Yourself

A career in advertising is exciting, but it is not for everyone. 1) Do you have the imagination to think up ideas for an advertising campaign? 2) Can you work under pressure? 3) Are you good at writing and could you design a copy layout?

CHAPTER 5

SPECIALTY SALES

Specialty sales include products such as computers, farm equipment, and medical supplies, and such services as real estate, insurance, and investment programs. Specialty salespeople often make presentations to explain or demonstrate their product or service to potential buyers.

Computer Sales

Computer salespeople help customers buy the hardware (computer, printer, and other equipment) and the software (computer programs) that best suit their needs. Salespeople in electronics retail stores who understand the use of computers may not need a specialized education.

Most computer sales are made to customers such as the U.S. government, state governments, airlines, insurance companies, banks, telephone companies, and manufacturers. To sell computers to these specialty markets, you need advanced education.

43

Specialty salespeople often demonstrate their product.

Yee Vang works for a national computer manufacturer. Yee sold personal computers at a Radio Shack store while taking evening courses in business, accounting, marketing, and speech.

Computer technology is always changing, so Yee receives frequent update training courses. She works closely with the company engineers to prepare individual sales proposals. She has the writing skills needed for preparing technical proposals.

"I seldom see a customer," Yee says. "I send the proposal to the customer and follow up with phone calls. Twice a year, I attend a computer trade show where I demonstrate hardware and software. I meet potential customers and find out what kinds of new software would interest them."

Opportunities in computer sales continue to grow with computer use and technology. Salespeople earn $29,000 to more than $55,000 annually.

If you have good math and science skills and enjoy working with computers, you may want to prepare for a job like Yee's. Take advanced math, science, and computer courses to prepare for college. Get a job selling computers in a retail store.

Real Estate Sales

Jim McGillis is a real estate agent in St. Paul, Minnesota. Jim gets listings of homes that are for sale from the agency where he works. He shows the listed homes to potential buyers.

"I work on commission," Jim says. "When I sell a house, I get a percentage of the selling price. If another agent sells one of my listings, I also get a percentage, but I make more money on my own listings."

Many laws and regulations govern real estate sales. Most states require a test to obtain a real estate agent's license. Federal, state, and local laws that affect real estate change frequently. The prices of houses, land, and other property also fluctuate. Real estate agents must stay current by studying information from the National Association of Realtors.

Real estate agents generally work at an office during the day and show homes at night or on the weekends.

Some real estate agents are high school graduates. Others, like Jim, have studied real estate at a business school or community college or through correspondence courses at home.

Jim attends weekly meetings of the Rotary and Kiwanis clubs to meet people who may want to sell their home and buy a larger house. He spends part of each day in the office. Sometimes he makes cold calls in person or by phone. One weekend each month, he advertises for the public to come to an "open house" at one of his listings.

"I work during the day, but I show homes mostly during evenings, weekends, and holidays," Jim says. "People do not have time to look at homes during the week."

Sometimes I spend many hours showing homes to one family," Jim says. "If they decide to buy a house I show them, I start filling out papers. Math is important in completing the forms buyers sign when they agree to buy a house or apply for loan to pay for the house. If they cannot borrow enough money, I try to sell them a cheaper house, but get a lower commission. Or I might lose the sale."

Beginning real estate agents should be prepared for the drawbacks of this profession. Showing houses to people who work Monday through Friday means many hours put in on evenings and weekends. Also weeks or months may go by without a sale. Full-time real estate agents make between $19,000 and $50,000 a year or more, depending on experience and level of commission.

You can write to the National Association of Realtors for information about a real estate career. Ask several real estate agents in your community to tell you about their work.

Insurance Sales

Insurance agents also make specialty sales. Lucia Moreno sells health, home, and auto insurance policies for an insurance agency. Lucia's math skills and insurance courses helped her pass the state test for an insurance license.

Lucia gets leads—names of prospective buyers

—from her employer and by making cold calls. She makes appointments to interview prospective clients in their homes or offices. With information from the interview, she designs an insurance plan for the client. In a follow-up appointment, she explains the plan and tries to persuade the person to buy the insurance. For each policy she sells, Lucia receives commissions every year the client keeps the policy. She also services policies by answering clients' questions about billing, changing, or updating policies.

Beginning insurance agents often receive a base salary plus commission. Several years later, they earn commissions only. The average income for agents in their first year of selling is about $25,000. The average income after five years is $75,000.

Other Specialty Sales
People in specialty sales jobs sell medical supplies to doctors, clinics, and hospitals. Some sell office machines to businesses or large machinery to construction companies, farmers, and factories.

Questions to Ask Yourself
There are many opportunities open in specialty sales careers. 1) Which specialty sales career appeals to you and why? 2) What skills are necessary to be successful in specialty sales positions?

CHAPTER 6

DIRECT SALES

Early in American history, peddlers went from house to house selling such items as pots, pans, ribbons, and cloth. Today, people like Becky Fisher continue the direct sales tradition. Becky is a Quick Cuisine dealer. She demonstrates and sells cookware in people's homes.

"I went to a Quick Cuisine demonstration and liked the cookware," Becky explains. "So I hosted a home party and invited fifteen friends. When I saw how much they bought, I decided to sell the products myself. Three of my friends booked parties to help me get started."

Becky bought a starter sales kit for $300. A Quick Cuisine manager showed Becky how to fill out the paperwork and went along to her first demonstration.

Most home parties are held evenings or Saturdays. At each party, Becky explains the use of the products and cooks several dishes with

49

them. She answers customers' questions, urges them to place an order, book a home party, and consider selling Quick Cuisine. Most people do order, and usually at least one books a party. When Becky recruits five new dealers she will become a manager and receive a commission on their sales as well as her own.

Becky collects payment with each order. At the end of the evening, she uses a calculator to add up sales. She tells the hostess what bonus products she earned with the party sales.

Becky works from one to four evenings a week and some Saturdays. Her work time includes traveling to and from home parties, but she does not have to deliver the products. They are shipped to the party hostesses.

Becky sends the payments to Quick Cuisine with the orders. Once a month, the company sends her a commission check. Becky may earn a little more than minimum wage at a party with low sales. At a successful party, she earns $20 an hour or more. Becky pays self-employment tax and income tax on her commissions.

Do you enjoy telling people about a product? Do you have a reliable car? Are you persuasive and well-groomed? If you answer yes, you might succeed in direct sales.

Mary Kay cosmetics, Undercover Wear lingerie, Tupperware kitchen items, and Home Interiors decorations are some of the products

sold through home party plans. Avon representatives sell cosmetics to friends, relatives, and coworkers as well as door-to-door. To learn more about direct sales, look for these companies in the phone book. Call and ask to speak to a sales representative.

Questions to Ask Yourself

Direct sales can be a good way for you to explore the world of sales while working for yourself. However, in order to be successful, you must consider this career option carefully. 1) What kind of product do you think you would sell best? 2) How can you best find people to whom to sell your product? 3) Do you have the self-motivation necessary for such a job?

CHAPTER 7

GETTING THE JOB

Do you have the personality and character-istics for a successful sales career? To help yourself learn the answer, try this quiz. On a separate sheet of paper, write the letter of the sentence that best describes you in each set of statements.

1. a) I like to find out information and tell it to people.
    b) If I don't know something, I usually don't bother looking for the answer.
    c) If people want to tell me something, I'll listen.
2. a) When I meet a person, I ask questions to help me get to know her.
    b) I would rather be alone than listen to people talking.
    c) I like to listen to people because they are interesting.

Depending on your answers to the quiz, you may enjoy telemarketing.

3. a) When there is work to do, I get it done.
   b) There are more interesting things to do than work.
   c) If I know what needs to be done, I usually do it without being told.
4. a) My friends usually do what I suggest.
   b) It seems that no one really listens to me.
   c) I would rather work out an agreement with my friends than insist on having my own way.
5. a) I don't need a calculator to add a few numbers.
   b) Math has always been a problem for me.
   c) I can solve some math problems in my head, but a calculator is handy.
6. a) When I want something to happen, I keep trying to make it happen until it does.
   b) If things don't go right, I usually give up and find something else to do.
   c) My answer could be a) or b), depending on my mood.
7. a) I have been successful in selling tickets, candy bars or another item in a fundraiser for school, YMCA, or Scouts.
   b) Asking someone to buy something makes me uncomfortable.
   c) If I think something is a good deal, I don't mind telling people about it.

Now add up your score. Give yourself two points for every "a" answer and one point for each "c" answer. Give yourself no points for "b" answers.

The highest score you can have is 14. If you have 11 or more points, you probably have natural talent for sales. Read the suggestions below under "Looking for Opportunities."

If your score is between 7 and 10, you probably can succeed in sales, but you will have to work hard. In Chapter 2 find the sales career you think is most interesting. Ask someone who has that career if you can "shadow" him or her for a few days. You will learn what sales work is like from day to day.

If you scored 6 or lower, sales is probably not the career for you. Your personality and interests are more suited to another kind of career.

Looking for Opportunities

If you scored 11 to 14 points on the quiz, take a good look at the sales careers in Chapter 2. Follow the suggestions, such as getting a part-time sales job and talking with people who have sales careers.

Join a DECA chapter if your school has one. Many high schools and junior colleges offer DECA courses in cooperation with local businesses. Under this program, a student goes to school half a day and spends the other half gaining experience at work. The student is paid while learning on the job.

Read the classified advertisements in your

If there is a certain store in which you would like to work, don't wait for an advertisement. Fill out an application. They may have an opening.

newspaper. Pay special attention to jobs listed under sales or marketing. You will get a good idea of the jobs in your area and what they pay.

Most retail businesses hire extra employees six or eight weeks before Christmas. Look for "seasonal help wanted" advertisements in the newspaper. If there is a certain store in which you would like to work, do not wait to see an advertisement. Fill out an application at the store in October. Start looking for a summer job in April. You will have a better chance of getting the job you want.

Wear clean, neat clothes when applying for a

job. Do not wear flashy clothes. Make sure your hair, face, hands, and nails are clean and neat.

You will need certain information when you fill out a job application. Be sure you have your Social Security number and your parents' address and phone number if you do not live with them. You may also need the name and address of a relative who does not live with you. You may be asked to list as references three people who know you well but are not related to you. You might choose a neighbor, a teacher, and the parent of a friend. Ask for permission to use their names before you apply for a job.

Meeting Your Goals and Getting the Job

Even if you have already made the decision to have a career in sales, you may still be uncertain about what it takes to get the job you want. What are employers looking for?

Preparation and enthusiasm are two key factors in getting a job. So do a little homework. The best way to find out about a job is to ask someone who works in the sales position that interests you. See what this person likes about the job and what the drawbacks might be. Be specific, but not nosy. Many people consider it rude to be asked how much money they make. Most people will, however, be glad to tell you about their everyday activities and about what they truly enjoy in their profession. Sometimes finding a person to talk to is difficult, but you may also be able to find the information in your library. Research the particular job you like.

Another way to be prepared is to start early. If you know you're interested in sales, or would like to learn more about it, take some business-related classes. Also try to think of some practical courses that could help you. For example, if you are thinking about a job in fashion retailing, take an art design or sewing class.

Previous work experience is also appealing to many employers. You can even try volunteer jobs or activities. For instance, selling ads for your school newspaper or yearbook may help you get a job in print media advertising.

Education and experience on any résumé will give you a better chance of getting that job.

Questions to Ask Yourself

Like all careers, a career in sales requires preparation and careful consideration. 1) What kind of personality and characteristics are necessary for a successful career in sales? 2) What can you do now to help yourself get a job in the future? 3) How can you get experience in sales?

GLOSSARY

advertising Public announcement to sell or promote a product or service.

bonus Money awarded to a person who makes exceptionally large sales.

cold calls Telephone calls or door-to-door sales visits to people who are not prior customers.

commission Payment to a salesperson based on a percentage of the sale.

consignee Person who brings merchandise to a store to be sold on contract with the owner.

consumer Person who buys and uses products and services; a customer.

discount Reduction in the price of a product or service.

incentive A reason for exerting greater effort.

inventory The products, materials, and property of a business.

listings In real estate, homes that are listed for sale.

media (singular, **medium**) Printed or electronic means of communication.

APPENDIX

Sales and Marketing Organizations

American Marketing Association
250 South Wacker Drive, Suite 200
Chicago, IL 60606
Web site: http://www.ama.org/

Direct Marketing Association
11 West 42nd Street
New York, NY 10036-8096
Web site: http://www.thefldma.org/

Direct Marketing Educational Foundation
6 East 43rd Street
New York, NY 10017-4646

Direct Selling Association
1666 K Street NW, Suite 1010
Washington, DC 20006
Web site: http://www.dsa.org

Distributive Education Clubs of America (DECA)
1908 Association Drive
Reston, VA 22090

Marketing Research Association
2189 Silar Deane Highway, Suite 5
Rocky Hill, CT 06067
Web site: http://www.mraflnet.org/

National Association of General Merchandise Representatives
401 North Michigan Avenue
Chicago, IL 60611-4267

National Association of Realtors
430 North Michigan Avenue
Chicago, IL 60611-4087
Web site: http.www.realtor.com/

National Federation of Independent Businesses
Division of Education
53 Century Boulevard
Nashville, TN 37214-3693

National Retail Federation—Careers
100 West 31st Street
New York, NY 10001
Web site: http://www.nrf.com/

General Sales/Marketing Magazines and Newsletters

Income Opportunities
1500 Broadway
New York, NY 10036-4015

Professional Selling and
Sales Manager's Bulletin
The Bureau of Business Practice
24 Rope Ferry Road
Waterford, CT 06386

FOR FURTHER READING

Barrett, Linda. *Sales and Distribution.* New York: Franklin Watts, 1991.

Basye, Anne. *Opportunities in Direct Marketing Careers.* Lincolnwood, IL: VGM Career Horizons, 1993.

————. *Opportunities in Telemarketing Careers.* Lincolnwood, IL: VGM Career Horizons, 1994.

Drahm, Ralph M., and Brescoll, James. *Opportunities in Sales Careers.* Lincolnwood, IL: VGM Career Horizons, 1988.

Dolber, Roslyn. *Opportunities in Fashion Careers.* Lincolnwood, IL: VGM Career Horizons, 1994.

Epstein, Lawrence. *Exploring Careers in Computer Sales.* New York: The Rosen Publishing Group, 1990.

Koester, Pat. *Careers in Fashion Retailing.* New York: The Rosen Publishing Group, 1990.

Occupational Outlook Handbook. Washington, DC: U.S. Department of Labor, 1996.

INDEX

About the Author

Carlienne Frisch has written books on such diverse topics as pet care, European countries, and the author Maud Hart Lovelace. Before becoming a freelance writer, she worked as an editor for a farm magazine and in public relations for nonprofit organizations.

Ms. Frisch is president of the Friends of the Minnesota Valley Regional Library and a member of the Society of Children's Book Writers, Habitat for Humanity, and the local historical society.

Ms. Frisch and her husband, Robert, have four adult children and a young granddaughter.

PHOTO CREDITS: Cover, pp. 2, 9, 20 © Gary Gladstone/Image Bank; p. 17 © Larry Gatz/Image Bank; p. 24 © Steve Dunwell/ Image Bank; p. 28 © Alvis Upitis/Image Bank; p. 39 © Lou Jones/ Image Bank; p. 43 © Steve Niedorf/Image Bank; all other photos © AP/Wide World Photos.
PHOTO RESEARCH: Vera Ahmadzadeh
DESIGN: Kim Sonsky